The Orinoco River

The Orinoco River

Carol B. Rawlins

Franklin Watts
A Division of Grolier Publishing
New York • London • Hong Kong • Sydney
Danbury, Connecticut

*For my daughter, Carol Williams, and my son, Bruce Frey.
They bring me joy.*

Note to readers: Definitions for words in **bold** can be found in the Glossary at the back of this book.

Photographs ©: Aurora & Quanta Productions: 21 (Robert Canuto); Corbis-Bettmann: 48; D. Donne Bryant Stock Photography: 12, 13, 50, 52 (R. Perron), 15 (Chris R. Sharp), 27, 40, 41; David Johnson: 45; H. Armstrong Roberts, Inc.: 5 top, 36 (Geopress), 18 (George Hunter); Kevin Schafer: 46 (Martha Hill), 14; Panos Pictures: 31 (Arabella Cecil), 6, 22, 28, 38 (Alfredo Cedeño); Robert Perron: cover; 9; South American Pictures: 23, 24, 32, 49, 51 (Tony Morrison); Superstock, Inc.: 8, 30, 34; Tony Stone Images: 16 (Ken Fisher), 5 bottom, 26 (Jaques Jangoux), 2 (Joel Simon); Viesti Collection, Inc.: 42 (Degas Parra).

Map by Bob Italiano.

Visit Franklin Watts on the Internet at:
http://publishing.grolier.com

Library of Congress Cataloging-in-Publication Data

Rawlins, Carol.
    The Orinoco River / Carol B. Rawlins
        p.   cm.— (Watts library)
    Includes bibliographical references and index.
    Summary: Examines the location, origin, history, and uses of the Orinoco River.
    ISBN: 0-531-11740-5 (lib. bdg.)   0-531-16429-2 (pbk.)
    1. Orinoco River (Venezuela and Colombia)—Juvenile literature. [1. Orinoco River (Venezuela and Colombia)] I. Title. II. Series.
F2331.O7R38 1999
987.06'33—dc21   99-10816
                                                                              CIP

Contents

Chapter One
A River Comes of Age   7

Chapter Two
Venezuela—Home of the Orinoco   11

Chapter Three
The Orinoco Drainage Area   19

Chapter Four
A Highway to the Interior   25

Chapter Five
The River's Source   29

Chapter Six
The Upper River   37

Chapter Seven
The Lower River   43

Chapter Eight
The Orinoco Delta   51

54   **Glossary**

57   **To Find Out More**

59   **A Note On Sources**

61   **Index**

A Warao Indian mother and daughter wash their clothes with water from the Orinoco River.

Chapter One

A River Comes of Age

A young Warao Indian woman carries her laundry to the edge of the river. She hopes to get a good start before the sun rises any higher and the day becomes too hot. The woman and her family, along with their dogs and a few chickens, live on a tiny rain forest island in the mouth of Venezuela's Orinoco River.

On this end-of-summer February day, the river is low. Dredges work steadily to keep the river channels deep enough for ocean freighters to pass. A remote

The industrial complex on the lower Orinoco River has brought many aspects of modern life to the Warao.

New Industrial Complex

Everything that is needed for manufacturing—raw materials, electric power, a sufficient labor force, and transportation—is brought together at Guayana City on the lower river.

rain forest river just forty years ago, the Orinoco River is now the lifeline for a new **industrial** complex along the lower river. An oceangoing freighter was a rare sight for the grandmother of the young Warao woman, but this woman sees them often.

Upside-Down Seasons

Summer arrives in the Northern Hemisphere, which is north of the equator, when Earth's north pole tilts toward the sun. This occurs every June 21. Six months later, on December 21, Earth's orbit has taken it to the other side of the sun. Now it is the south pole that tilts toward the sun. At that time, summer comes to the Southern Hemisphere, which is south of the equator.

Canoe People

The Warao people live in the **delta** region of the Orinoco River. "Warao" means "canoe people." The Warao learn to swim and paddle canoes almost before they can walk. They fish in the river, grow rice, work in agriculture, and hunt. They are known for their fine dugout canoes, hammocks, basketry, and wood carving. The Warao know the river well. "Orinoco" is a Warao word meaning "father of our land" or "a place to paddle." The Orinoco River is the third-largest of the many great rivers crisscrossing the South American continent.

An aerial view of the Orinoco River, which flows for 1,300 miles (2,092 kilometers) across South America.

Continents

Continents are the six or seven great divisions of land on Earth: Africa, Antarctica, Australia, North America, South America, Europe, and Asia. Sometimes Europe and Asia are combined as Eurasia.

ATLANTIC OCEAN

CARIBBEAN SEA

SOUTH AMERICA

N
W   E
S

Gulf of Paria

★ Caracas

Orinoco Delta

Lake Maracaibo

The Llanos

Orinoco River

Guayana City

△ Pico Bolívar

Bolívar City

Apure River

Caicara del Orinoco

Guri Dam

VENEZUELA

Andes Mountains

Caura River

Canaima National Park

Caroní River

Angel Falls

Meta River

Atures Rapids

Port Ayacucho

Ventuari River

La Gran Sabana

GUYANA

Maipures Rapids

Samariapo

Guiana Highlands

COLOMBIA

San Fernando de Atabapo

Orinoco River

La Esmeralda

Sierra Parima

Guaviare River

Casiquiare Channel

Amazon Basin

Negro River

BRAZIL

KEY
⌒ Dam
≢ Rapids

Note: Lighter area shows the Orinoco River Basin.

0   200 Miles

0   200 Kilometers

Chapter Two

Venezuela— Home of the Orinoco

The Orinoco River is one of the five largest river systems in South America. The entire 1,300-mile (2,092-kilometer) course of the river lies within Venezuela, the sixth-largest and northernmost country in South America. With an area of about 352,000 square miles (912,000 square km), Venezuela is about the size of the U.S. states of Texas and Oklahoma combined.

North of Venezuela lies the Caribbean Sea, and to the northeast, the Atlantic Ocean. Venezuela's neighbors are Colombia to the west, Brazil to the south, and Guyana to the east. The world's largest rain forest, the great Amazon region, covers the southern part of Venezuela and extends into Colombia and Brazil.

From the Coast to the Mountains

Low mountain ranges lie south of the beautiful beaches along Venezuela's Caribbean coastline. The mountains become higher as they extend in an east-west arc to the Andes Mountains in the west. Pico Bolívar, at 16,427 feet (5,007 meters), is Venezuela's highest peak. Some peaks remain snowcovered throughout the year.

The Andes Mountains, which extend 4,500 miles (7,242 km) down the western coast of South America, form a "Y" in Venezuela. Lake Maracaibo, the largest lake in South America and Venezuela's major oil-producing area, lies within the wide part of the "Y." Until the 1960s, oil exports from Lake Maracaibo were Venezuela's primary source of wealth.

12

Wide, low valleys lie between the coastal mountains and the Andes Mountains in the west. Two-thirds of the people of Venezuela live in the fertile mountain valleys where the temperatures are more moderate. Caracas, Venezuela's capital city of three million people, is located in a mountain valley, along with most of Venezuela's industry and agriculture.

Pico Bolívar, Venezuela's highest peak

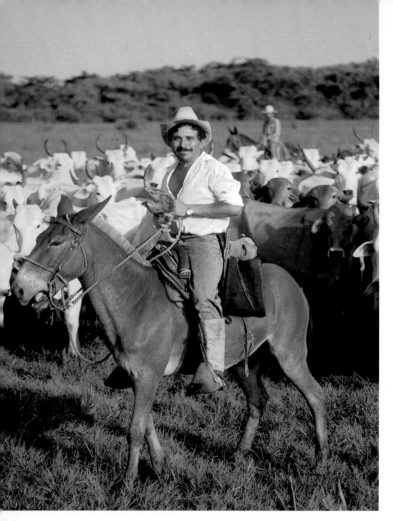

A llanero, *or plains-man, tends cattle on the llanos, Venezuela's vast plains.*

Venezuela's Great Plains

South of the coastal mountains and east of the higher Andes Mountains lie vast, almost treeless, grassy plains. The Orinoco River flows along the southern edge of the plains on the eastward leg of its journey to the ocean.

The llanos, the Spanish word for the plains, cover one-third of Venezuela. Yearly flooding, followed by **drought** and extreme temperatures mean that the llanos have been left largely to herds of cattle and to the *llaneros*, or plains-men, who tend them.

Highlands and Tepuis

The Guiana Highlands south of the Orinoco River are exactly that—high lands. The Guiana Highlands are what remains of an ancient landform called the Guayana Shield. The Guayana Shield was once part of a much larger continent from which the South American continent broke off.

The Guiana Highlands cover about one-half of Venezuela. The region is composed of two distinct geological regions. In the southwestern section is a hot, damp, tropical rain forest called the Amazonas Territory. Venezuela's Amazon region is the northern extension of the great Amazon territory of Brazil and Colombia.

East of the Amazonas Territory lies the Gran Sabana (Great Savanna). This vast grassy highland is located in the basin of the Caroní River. The Caroní is the Orinoco's largest **tributary**.

Rising above the highlands are a hundred or more gigantic *tepuis*. *Tepuis* are flat-topped mountains with steep vertical

Many of Venezuela's tepuis *are so remote, they have never been explored.*

World's Tallest

Angel Falls drops 3,212 feet (980 meters) over Auyán-tepuí. The falls are fifteen times as high as Niagara Falls, located between the United States and Canada. The falls were named for Jimmy Angel, an American prospector and pilot who first spotted the falls from the air in 1935. Angel later died after a plane crash near the falls.

sides. Called the "houses of the gods" by the Pemon Indians who inhabit the region, *tepuis* are usually impossible to climb. Most have never been explored. Until 1990, when a highway was constructed into the Gran Sabana, the region was accessible only by air or by river and backpacking.

Venezuela has an extensive network of national parks and forest preserves. Many of the protected areas lie within the Guiana Highlands. Best known is Canaima National Park, famous for Angel Falls, the world's tallest free-falling waterfall.

Climate and People

Venezuela is near the equator, so its **climate** is tropical. Temperatures in the lowlands are always mild, though temperatures drop as elevation increases. Venezuela's two seasons are marked by rainfall differences rather than by temperature changes. Its seasons are the opposite of those in North America. Winter, a long rainy season, is from May through October or November. Summer, the dry season, is from December through April. Most of the country has a rainy season, though rainfall varies in different locations.

Venezuela's population of about 21 million is 2 percent Indian (native to the region), 8 percent black (descendants of African slaves), 20 percent white (descendants of European settlers or more recent immigrants), and 70 percent mestizo (any combination of Indian, European, or African ancestry).

The Atlantic Ocean is one of the world's four major bodies of water.

Chapter Three

The Orinoco Drainage Area

The world's oceans and seas are at low points, called sea level, on Earth's surface. All running water not absorbed into the ground—whether from rainfall, melting snow, or your bathtub—eventually makes its way downhill to one of these vast bodies of water.

Streams and rivers are part of this distribution system. They collect the runoff from a certain geographical area and then move that water from stream to river until it reaches the channel of a primary river. Primary rivers deliver their water to the nearest sea or ocean. The Orinoco River is a primary river because it flows into the Atlantic Ocean.

The River Basin

The Orinoco River and its tributaries drain an area slightly larger than Venezuela. The Orinoco **drainage area** includes the eastern slopes of the Andes Mountains, the llanos region of Colombia, and three-quarters of the Venezuelan states.

The Orinoco River Basin includes 385,000 square miles (997,000 sq km). "Basin" refers to the bowl shape of the land surrounding a river. During the rainy season each year, the Orinoco River and its more than four hundred tributaries overflow their banks, flooding much of the Orinoco River Basin. Between June and August, some low places in the basin are 65 feet (20 m) under water.

The average depth of the Orinoco River near Bolívar City, on the lower river, is 49 feet (15 m) during the dry season. During the peak of the rainy season, the Orinoco River is as much as 165 feet (50 m) deep in the same place.

Isolation Ends

Many of the great civilizations in history grew up along the banks of rivers. But with the exception of the population of Bolívar City on the lower river, throughout its history, the vast Orinoco River Basin has been home to relatively few people.

The small communities of indigenous people who lived near the streams and rivers in the Orinoco Basin at times were joined by a few **subsistence farmers,** plantation workers, and *llaneros.* Occasionally, some prospectors, timbermen, traders,

A view of Bolívar City, with the Orinoco River in the background

Construction of the Guri Dam, which provides hydroelectric power to the industrial complex on the lower Orinoco River

missionaries, and a few others who preferred isolation passed through, but their numbers were never great.

Now, however, the isolation of the Orinoco River is coming to an end. Knowing that its supplies of petroleum in the north would someday be used up, the Venezuelan government determined to develop the country's natural resources. In the 1960s, the government began construction of an industrial complex on the lower Orinoco River. The region is rich in various ores, water power, trees, and lower grades of oil, which have industrial use. New highways connect cities in the north to the industrial center. Hydroelectric plants, which use water power to generate electricity, at the Macagua and the Guri dams on the Caroní River provide power for the new industry.

A Pristine River

The Orinoco is still **pristine,** a rare condition for the rivers of industrialized nations. River experts are studying the Orinoco to learn more about the relationship of the river to the land it drains. The quality of the Orinoco's water has not yet been significantly altered by waste from industry and human development.

Life in the Amazon rain forest comes in many forms. Some species of trees and plants in the Amazon appear to depend upon the annual floods of the rain forest rivers to support their life cycles. The lush growth in the rain forests contributes oxygen to Earth's atmosphere and absorbs carbon dioxide. People and animals need these conditions in order to survive. We do not know all the ways that the **diversity** of the rain forests contributes to the survival of life on this planet, but we do know that diversity is important.

Rain clouds hang in the trees of South America's Amazon rain forest.

None Flows West

South America's Amazon, Plata Paraná, and Orinoco rivers all empty into the Atlantic Ocean on the eastern coast of the continent. Strangely, none flows west.

The Andes Mountains cause the lopsided drainage pattern. Millions of years ago the Amazon River actually did flow west to empty into the Pacific Ocean. But that was before the Andes Mountains were forced upward by pressure from under the Earth. When the mountains emerged, the Amazon River was forced to change its course and flow east.

Christopher Columbus reached the coast of South America in 1498.

Chapter Four

A Highway to the Interior

Long before the Europeans arrived, ancient Indian people in long canoes used the Orinoco River to travel great distances. The Yekwana people, who live near the upper Orinoco River, are descendants of the Carib people who inhabit the Caribbean islands off the coast of Venezuela. The similar language of the two separated groups reveals that their ancestors traveled the 1,700 miles (2,736 km) between the upper Orinoco and the islands.

European Explorers

On Christopher Columbus's third voyage to the New World in 1498, he reached the mainland of South America. He sailed along the Venezuelan coast and explored the delta of the Orinoco River. Awestruck by the vast amount of freshwater, the lush green forests, and the graceful people decorated with pearls, Columbus wrote that he had found an "Earthly Paradise."

Another Spanish explorer, Alonso de Ojeda, explored the northern coast of Venezuela in 1499. Ojeda found salt deposits and pearl beds. He named the land Venezuela, "Little Venice." Ojeda was the first Spaniard to sail up the Orinoco River.

Black Gold

Alonso de Ojeda's ships anchored in Lake Maracaibo in 1499. The sailors caulked their ships with a thick black substance they found in the water. The substance was oil. They took samples back to Spain. At first, little use was found for oil, but later, in the form of kerosene, oil replaced whale oil as the preferred fuel for lamps. In the twentieth century, the oil in Lake Maracaibo made Venezuela a wealthy nation.

In 1800, Alexander von Humboldt, a German naturalist, explored the entire length of the Orinoco River. His party traveled into the Casiquiare Channel, a unique natural channel that links the Orinoco and Amazon rivers. Humboldt also explored the Amazon River system. He made extensive notes and drawings of the landmarks and plant and animal life. His extensive journals, written between 1800 and 1805, inspired later generations of Europeans to seek the source of the Orinoco. However, the beginning of the river remained elusive for another 150 years.

Today's Explorers

Modern explorers of the interior of South America are scientists, environmentalists, developers, and tourists. In spite of the construction of major highways in Venezuela in recent years, the more remote parts of the country remain isolated. The Orinoco River continues to be the major highway into the interior.

Despite modern developments along the river, many unspoiled areas can still be enjoyed by visitors.

An aerial view of the rain forest where the source of the Orinoco River lies

Chapter Five

The River's Source

In 1952, a team of explorers from Venezuela and France finally reached the **headwaters** of the Orinoco River. The river begins as a mountain stream 3,500 feet (1,067 m) up in southern Venezuela's Sierra Parima, in a region known as the Amazonas Territory. The Amazonas Territory includes one-fifth of all of the land in Venezuela, but only one percent of the people. The land is covered with some of the densest rain forest in the world. Only occasionally are the thick trees broken by small clearings. The many rivers and streams that meander through the thick forests are the primary routes for travel.

The Amazonas Territory has a typical rain forest climate: warm and humid. Light rain falls even in the dry season. During the rainy season, rainfall is so heavy that mountain torrents and rapids pour into the Orinoco River and its tributaries. The long rainy season leaves only a few months each year in which exploring parties can canoe and backpack into the region.

Explorers telling about their efforts to explore the upper Orinoco River describe mildew and mold that rotted their shoes, and wet clothing that never dried out. Metal equipment rusted quickly, becoming useless.

Keeping adequate food and supplies was a challenge for explorers. Though the many rivers were rich with fish, catching them was not easy. Piranha with razor-sharp teeth lay in wait, ready to strip the flesh from the bones of any catch not quickly yanked from the water.

Amazon parrots are pets to many of South America's indigenous people.

Animal and Plant Life

Though conditions surrounding the upper Orinoco River seem downright unfriendly to outsiders, the isolated region, with its greenhouselike climate, is perfectly suited to the unique animals and plants that are native to the region. Vividly colored parrots and monkeys with prehensile tails chatter overhead. People tell of darting hummingbirds, giant frogs with luminous green stripes, blue butterflies, and rare black orchids.

Anaconda snakes, some about 20 feet (6 m) long, hide among the **liana** vines, poised to drop down and knock their unlucky prey into the river to drown. Another snake, the

More Than a Tail

"Prehensile" means made for grasping. This word is used to describe the tails of certain animals, especially sloths, opposums, and some monkeys.

An Indian man with a captured anaconda

A tapir approaches a watering hole for a drink.

That's Shocking

The electric eel of the Amazon and Orinoco rivers produces electric shocks of six hundred volts. The voltage of the electric catfish and electric ray is much less powerful, and that of the stargazer fish and mormyrid eel is milder still.

bushmaster viper, grows as much as 12 feet (4 m) in length. Like the anaconda, it hides in the foliage overhead.

Tapirs with small elephant-like trunks weigh as much as 400 pounds (181 kilograms). A giant catfish, the laulao, lives on the dark bottoms of the rivers. The laulao weighs from 200 to 300 pounds (90 to 136 kg), but has been reported to be as large as 500 pounds (227 kg).

A species of electric eel in the linked Orinoco and Amazon rivers grows to be 6 feet (2 m) in length. It can produce electric shocks of six hundred volts, enough to stun a horse.

Valuable rubber and mahogany trees are just two of the more than one hundred species of trees in the rain forest. It is estimated that ninety-eight percent of the plants in the region have never been identified.

Indigenous People

Except for the Guajiro people of Lake Maracaibo in northwest Venezuela, all of Venezuela's indigenous communities inhabit the Orinoco River Basin. Each cultural group has its own language and customs. Some communities live in near-isolation. Others have more contact with outsiders.

The three main indigenous groups in Amazonas Territory are the Yanomami, the Piaroa, and the Guajibo. Some smaller groups make up the remaining native population.

The People of the River

The Yekwana, also called the Makiritare, are a small community known as "the people of the river." They have straight black hair and decorate themselves with colorful feathers and body paint.

The Yekwana hunt with bows and arrows and blowpipes. They build immense clay homes with 10-foot (3-m)-high ceilings. Using steel axes obtained from traders, they cut down trees to make canoes and clear areas to plant bananas, pineapples, yams, and cassava, whose roots are ground into flour. They bake bread, season their food, cook and cure game, and grind and grate their food, all indications that they have developed more complex ways than some of their neighbors who live more simply.

The Yekwana have more contact with outsiders than some other rain forest groups. They sometimes trade at regional trading posts. A few are taught by local missionaries. Others have contact with Venezuelan soldiers who maintain outposts downriver. The people are highly respected as river and overland guides by rubber or timber companies, missionaries, and explorers in the territory.

One visitor to the region commented that the Yekwana "transform" (change or improve) their environment, while their better-known neighbors, the Yanomami people, "suffer it" (just put up with it).

One of Venezuela's Yanomami Indians hunting with a bow and arrows.

The Fierce People

The Yanomami are the people most feared by outsiders and by the other indigenous groups in the Amazonas Territory. Sometimes referred to as "the fierce people," the Venezuelan Yanomami are part of the larger Yanomami group that extends into Brazil and Colombia.

The Yanomami have a **culture** built on confrontation. They have a rigid set of rules for behavior. Breaking the rules often leads to conflict within their own community and with outsiders.

The Yanomami are small people with an average height of 4 1/2 feet (1.4 m). Some wear their hair in a crown, with the tops of their heads shaved. They wear little clothing and decorate themselves with ceremonial paint.

The 6-foot (2-m)-long bows of the Yanomami are distinctive. The people eat peccaries, which are similar to pigs, and monkeys, which they kill with poisoned darts and arrows.

The Yanomami live in isolation deep within the thick rain forest. Their hostility to other indigenous groups and to outsiders is rooted in dark incidents from their past: Through the years, many were enslaved or massacred by members of foreign expeditions.

Biosphere Reserve

In 1991, the United Nations created the Upper Orinoco-Casiquiare Biosphere Reserve to protect the people and **ecosystem** of the region. Mining, logging, and other unnecessary intrusions by outsiders are restricted. No outsider is allowed into the Biosphere Reserve without government permission. The region is vast, however, and difficult to patrol, except by air, so the future of the region and its people remains uncertain.

Homes of Yekwana Indians located along the Orinoco in La Esmeralda.

Chapter Six

The Upper River

Small settlements occasionally sprang up along the upper river at locations where large rocks, beaches, or open spaces made a break in the thick trees lining the banks of the river. The old settlement of La Esmeralda, downriver from the Orinoco's source, is a favorite stopping place.

The Casiquiare Channel

The Orinoco River takes an unusual turn 30 miles (48 km) below La Esmeralda. Part of the river breaks away to turn

Canoeing along the Casiquiare Channel

Blue Mountain

From La Esmeralda, visitors can see the beautiful blue mountain, Mount Duida, with its cloud-covered summit. Back toward the source of the river, the black-purple peaks of the Sierra Parima rise in the distance. Brazil lies on the far side of the mountains.

south into the Casiquiare Channel, while the main part of the river continues north.

The Casiquiare Channel is a 220-mile (354-km) natural channel. It connects the yellow waters of the Orinoco River to the ink-black waters of the Negro River, a tributary of the Amazon River. The channel thus links the Orinoco River system to the Amazon River system. Together they form the world's largest river system. The Orinoco-Amazon system replenishes Earth's oceans, discharging one-quarter of the world's total supply of freshwater into the Atlantic Ocean.

Rarely is a river system connected to another river system across a watershed, as are the Amazon and Orinoco systems. A watershed is a natural dividing line. Water on one side of a watershed flows in one direction. On the other side, it flows in the opposite direction.

Observers wonder which way the water in the Casiquiare Channel actually flows. The dark water flowing up the channel from the Negro River appears to be dominant from time to time; other times, the yellow Orinoco, flowing down the channel, seems to be.

Beyond the Casiquiare Channel, as the Orinoco swings again toward the west, the Ventuari River joins it. Sandbars build up in the confluence, or joining place, of the two rivers. Other rivers join the Orinoco along its entire length. Some flow out of neighboring Colombia. Others are from within Venezuela.

Common Boundary with Colombia

The Orinoco turns northward and becomes the border between the countries of Venezuela and Colombia. There are army checkpoints on both sides of the river. Travelers stop at the settlement of San Fernando de Atabapo, Venezuela, to have their passports checked. The large Guaviare River joins the Orinoco from Colombia just beyond San Fernando de Atabapo. The Orinoco River is now about 1 mile (1.6 km) wide.

Region of the Rapids

The final 45-mile (73-km) stretch of common boundary between Colombia and Venezuela is known as *Región de los Raudales*, or the Region of the Rapids. The name of one set of rapids, *Raudales de Muerto*, or the Rapids of Death, indicates how the local people feel about this stretch of river.

Maipures Rapids is the first major barrier on the trip downriver. The river is forced between and over enormous granite boulders that create channels and non-navigable rapids. Travelers going downriver must leave the river above the rapids, near the town of Samariapo.

At Atures Rapids—the final, and most dangerous, set of rapids—the river travels over large, flat rocks and then drops, creating a waterfall. No one has ever taken a firm-sided boat through the rapids and lived. Recently, however, a British hovercraft successfully nav-

igated the rapids, and now soft-sided rubber rafts are offered to any tourist willing to risk his or her life running the rapids. The rapids are the only barrier to continuous river travel from the mouth of the Amazon River on the Atlantic Ocean in Brazil to Venezuela's Gulf of Paria near the Caribbean Sea.

Many visitors consider their trip to the rain forest incomplete without a whitewater rafting excursion down the Orinoco River.

Residents of Port Ayacucho use the river for recreation and refreshment on a hot summer day.

Chapter Seven

The Lower River

The town of Port Ayacucho, below the Atures Rapids, marks the halfway point on the river. A town of 100,000 people, Port Ayacucho is the government center for the upper river region. Officials at Port Ayacucho control access to Amazonas Territory. The town has a hospital, hotels, an airport, and other services.

Until recently, Port Ayacucho was accessible only by air or river. A newly built highway now connects Port Ayacucho with Caracas in the north and Bolívar City downriver.

Travelers board a steamer at Port Ayacucho for the remainder of the trip downriver. During the rainy season, the lower river is deep enough for large steamers to navigate as far upriver as Port Ayacucho. Larger ships are forced to stop at Bolívar City, where the river narrows to less than 1 mile (1.6 km) and rocks in the river restrict their movement.

Below Port Ayacucho, the Orinoco continues flowing north. The Orinoco is joined by the large Meta River, which flows out of Colombia from the west. The Meta River flows between western Venezuela and Colombia. Originating in the higher elevations of the Andes Mountains, the Meta River adds runoff from melting snow to the seasonal flooding of the Lower Orinoco Basin.

The Apure River, another tributary river, also joins the Orinoco from the west. The Orinoco is from 5 to 7 miles (8 to 11 km) wide after the two rivers join. At the confluence of the Orinoco and Apure rivers, the Orinoco swings toward the east as it begins the final leg of its journey to the ocean. The low, grassy llanos are north of the river. The rugged Guiana Highlands are south of the river.

The Llanos

The vast llanos are 1,000 miles (1,600 km) wide from west to east and 200 miles (320 km) at the widest point from north to south. Extreme temperatures and conditions keep the almost treeless plains low in population. The climate ranges from hot and dry to warm and muggy.

Severe drought from January to April is followed by seasonal flooding. During the rainy season, the many streams and rivers that cross the llanos overflow their banks. The llanos are at the lowest elevation in the Orinoco River Basin, so they receive the runoff from surrounding higher elevations. When the heavy rains cease, floodwaters recede, and rivers and streams return to their regular channels. The returning streams carry fertile soil lifted from more fertile areas farther away. The fertile **sediment** is deposited along the banks of the streams. Strips of trees are thus able to grow along the streams. Between the Apure River and Bolívar City, subsistence farmers grow seasonal crops.

Although irrigation and flood control programs have increased agricultural production of the llanos, they remain a difficult area to farm and few people live there.

New Breadbasket

Producing enough food to feed its rapidly growing population is a challenge for Venezuela. Recent irrigation and drainage projects on the western llanos increased acreage that can now be cultivated. The country's new "breadbasket" now produces two-thirds of the country's rice and one-half of its corn.

Llanos Giants

With more than 350 species of birds, the llanos are a birder's paradise. The grasslands are also the habitat of the world's largest rodent, the capybara, and the longest crocodile of its kind in the world. The capybara, with a face like a guinea pig, grows up to 4 feet (1 m) long and can weigh 160 pounds (73 kg). The Orinoco crocodile, about 20 feet (6 m) long, has been hunted almost to extinction for its hide. A smaller crocodile is found in greater numbers here.

Only nine percent of the people of Venezuela live on the llanos, along with five million cattle, horses, and donkeys first brought to Venezuela from Spain in the 1600s. The *llaneros* who tend the cattle drive them to drier areas during the rainy season. When the drought comes, they move the cattle to water. The courage and stamina of the fabled *llaneros* make them heroes of Venezuelan songs and stories. It is said that *llaneros* tend their cattle from canoes when the grasslands are flooded.

Caicara del Orinoco

Caicara del Orinoco, about halfway between Port Ayacucho and Bolívar City, was once an isolated stopping place on the south bank of the Orinoco River. The town is served now by newly built highways connecting it to Bolívar City downriver and to Port Ayacucho upriver.

Tributary rivers enter the main river from both the east and the west. The significant Caura River comes in from the east out of the Guiana Highlands. Small islands in the confluences of the entering rivers are plentiful and separate the Orinoco waters into narrow channels.

Nearing Bolívar City, the most important city on the Orinoco River, travelers pass under the only bridge across the Orinoco for its entire length. The suspension bridge was built in 1967 to serve the industrial expansion on the lower river. It connects Bolívar City on the south bank of the river with the town of Soledad across the river and points north.

Bolívar City

Bolívar City is the capital of Venezuela's largest state, Bolívar. Bolívar City is 260 miles (420 km) from the Atlantic Ocean. It has a population of 270,000 and is one of the two major cities on the lower Orinoco River.

Simón Bolívar (1783–1830) is one of South America's best-known historical figures.

Founded as Angostura by Spaniards in 1764, Bolívar City is situated at the narrowest point on the river. Angostura means "the narrows." During the rainy season, the river becomes deep here rather than wide. A difference of more than 115 feet (35 m) may occur in the depth of the river at Bolívar City between the rainy and dry seasons.

Angostura remained a quiet river port until Simón Bolívar arrived in 1817 to lead the War of Independence from Spain. Angostura was the provisional capital of Venezuela during the war years. In 1846, Angostura was renamed Bolívar City in honor of "El Libertador" (The Liberator), Simón Bolívar.

Downriver from Bolívar City, **lagoons** expand from the banks of the Orinoco River. The Caroní River joins the Orinoco River from the east, after crashing over an impressive waterfall.

El Libertador

Inspired by the American and French revolutionary wars, Venezuelans declared independence from Spain in 1811. Simón Bolívar, a wealthy colonist, and his armies finally defeated Spanish troops in 1821. He went on to help free Peru and Bolivia from Spanish rule, as well. The country of Bolivia was named for Simón Bolívar, as is the bolívar, Venezuela's unit of money.

Guayana City

Guayana City, on the south bank of the Orinoco near the mouth of the Caroní River, is Venezuela's fastest growing city. Located 60 miles (97 km) east of Bolívar City, Guayana City is unique among river towns. It did not expand gradually from a small settlement into a large city. This relatively new city was built in 1961 by the Venezuelan government.

Guayana City is part of a state-directed program of industrial development on the lower river. Government-owned steelworks, modern aluminum and bauxite refineries, and several large wood pulp and newsprint plants are located here. Large deposits of iron ore, oil, bauxite, and other raw materials are nearby.

Hydroelectricity is critical to the development of Venezuela's new industry. The large Caroní River, which drains the Gran Sabana of the Guiana Highlands, is the site of the new Guri Dam.

This industrial complex at Guayana City produces iron ore, paper, and aluminum.

An aerial view of the Guri Dam, which makes electricity possible for millions of Venezuelans.

The Guri Dam is Venezuela's largest single source of electricity and the world's fourth-largest producer of electricity. In 1960, only thirty percent of Venezuelans had access to electricity. Today, ninety-two percent do. The Guri Dam eventually will supply all the energy needs of Venezuela, as well as some of those of neighboring countries.

Officials had hoped that the new industrial and urban center would attract many of the workers crowded into Venezuela's northern cities. Migration to the lower river region has far exceeded their original goal. Guayana City was planned for a population of 300,000 but may have more than one million people by the year 2000.

Opposite: During the rainy Venezuelan winter, the Orinoco's waters often rise more than 40 feet (12 m) and flood the llanos.

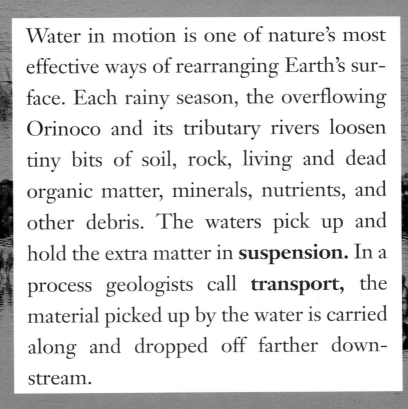

Chapter Eight

The Orinoco Delta

Water in motion is one of nature's most effective ways of rearranging Earth's surface. Each rainy season, the overflowing Orinoco and its tributary rivers loosen tiny bits of soil, rock, living and dead organic matter, minerals, nutrients, and other debris. The waters pick up and hold the extra matter in **suspension.** In a process geologists call **transport,** the material picked up by the water is carried along and dropped off farther downstream.

Islands and Deltas

As a stream or river joins a more powerful river, its current slows. The sediment it carries is released and sinks to the bottom of the river. Material builds up on the streambed until small islands are formed in the confluence of the two rivers. The same process created the great delta at the mouth of the Orinoco River. The Orinoco River slowed as it met the more powerful Atlantic Ocean. Its muddy load sank to the riverbed, gradually forming the great Orinoco Delta. Over time, the sediment has increased in volume. It now forms a 275-mile (443 km)-wide maze of islands.

The Orinoco Delta, where the river meets the Atlantic Ocean

The Orinoco Delta is one of the largest deltas in the world, and it continues to grow. The tangled roots of mangrove trees

on the banks of the islands help to trap mud and other materials. The river is 13 miles (21 km) wide as it reaches the delta. Near the town of Barrancas, the river is forced into more than one hundred channels between the islands. There are forty major channels through the delta. The channels are like the fingers of a wide-open hand.

The southernmost and main channel through the delta is the Rio Grande (Big River). Water in this channel flows into the Atlantic Ocean through its Boca Grande (Big Mouth). Oceangoing vessels travel upriver to Guayana City through the Rio Grande.

Delta Amacuro, the official name for the delta region, has a population of 104,000, of whom 24,000 are Warao Indians. The Warao are Venezuela's second-largest indigenous group.

The Future

Venezuela has little **arable** land and one of the highest rates of population growth in Latin America. The river delta is fertile, built from sediment lifted from fertile places along the length of the entire Orinoco River system. The government is attempting to make the marshy delta suitable for agriculture by building dikes to hold back the water.

The Orinoco's days as a remote river far from modern-day Venezuela are nearly finished. People concerned with preserving Earth's rivers hope the Orinoco's prized qualities can be retained, even as modern development comes to the Orinoco River Basin.

New Workforce

A British petroleum company is hiring the Warao for unskilled work in their new billion-dollar operation. The drilling rig is able to draw oil from the delta without disturbing Warao homelands. Some of the profits may go toward improving local living conditions.

Reclaiming Land

Some nations, such as The Netherlands, have been successful in reclaiming marshy land. Barriers or banks, called dikes, often constructed of earth, hold back the water. Dried-out land taken back from the mouth of a river, such as the Orinoco Delta, is often very fertile and suitable for agriculture.

Glossary

arable—fit for agriculture

climate—the usual weather in a place

culture—customary beliefs and behavior of a group of people

delta—deposit of sediment wherever a swift stream or river empties into a lake, ocean, or slower river

discharge—the amount of water a river empties into an adjoining body of water

diversity—variety

drainage area—the territory drained by a river and its tributaries

drought—a period without rainfall, which causes damage to crops

ecosystem—the relationship between plants and animals and their environment

headwaters—the source or beginning of a river

indigenous—native; belonging naturally to an area or region

industrial—related to manufacturing

lagoon—a shallow pond connecting to a larger body of water

lianas—woody climbing vines that use other plants for support to reach the light

pristine—fresh, clean, pure; without pollution

sediment—particles of soil that settle to the bottom of a river or stream

subsistence farmers—farmers who grow only enough food for their families to eat; there is no excess to sell

suspension—particles mixed in a liquid, but not dissolved

transport—the process of transferring or carrying river material from one place to another

tributary—a stream or river flowing into a larger stream or river

To Find Out More

Books (Non-Fiction)

Fox, Geoffrey. *The Land and People of Venezuela*. New York: HarperCollins, 1991.

Morrison, Marion. *Venezuela*. Chicago: Childrens Press, 1989.

Petersen, David. *South America*. Danbury, CT: Children's Press, 1998

Sayre, April Pulley. *South America*. New York: Twenty-First Century Books, 1999.

Venezuela . . . in Pictures. Minneapolis: Lerner Publications, 1987.

Winter, Jane Kohen. *Venezuela*. Tarrytown, NY: Marshall Cavendish, 1991.

Books (Fiction)

DeFoe, Daniel. *Robinson Crusoe*. Philadelphia: Running Press Book Publishers, 1990.

Doyle, Sir Arthur Conan. *The Lost World*. New York: Looking Glass Library, 1959.

Hudson, W. H. *Green Mansions*. New York: Random House, 1944.

L'Engle, Madeleine. *Dragons in the Waters*. New York: Farrar Straus Giroux, 1976.

Television

"Amazon: Land of the Flooded Forest." *World of National Geographic*.

"Warriors of the Amazon." *Nova* (PBS). (Features the Yanomami)

"World's Greatest Stunts." Discovery Channel. (Includes a parachutist over Angel Falls)

"Edge of the World." Travel Channel.

Organizations and Online Sites

Exploring Venezuela's Orinoco
http://www.gaia.earthwatch.org/g/Grjaffe.html
Sponsored by the Earthwatch Institute, this site contains the results of an extensive study of the upper Orinoco River.

Rainforest Alliance
65 Bleecker Street
New York, NY 10012
E-mail: canopy@ra.org
http://www.rainforest-alliance.org
This nonprofit international organization is dedicated to the conservation of tropical forests. Here you can read about the conservation programs it supports and review activities for students and teachers.

Venezuela: A Country Study
http://www.lcweb2.loc.gov/frd/cs/vetoc.html
Sponsored by the U.S. Library of Congress, this is a good place to start learning about Venezuela. The site contains sections on geography, history, society, economy, and more.

Venezuela Yours
http://www.venezuelatuya.com
Written in English, Spanish, and French, this site contains maps, photos, and descriptions of many cities and regions in Venezuela, including the Gran Sabana.

A Note On Sources

One of my favorite ways to find out about other countries is through the country studies series published by the federal government. So, for this book, I checked out *Venezuela: A Country Study. Venezuela*, by Marion Morrison, and *Venezuela*, by Jane Kohen Winter, are also good sources.

Finding out about the upper Orinoco River, which is relatively unexplored, was more difficult. I had to play detective. Journals of trips were a good place to start. My favorites were *Journey to the Far Amazon*, by Alain Gheerbrandt, and *The Last Great Journey on Earth*, by Brian Branston. Two fine guidebooks for travelers provided detailed information about towns and conditions along the river, especially *Venezuela: A Travel Survival Kit*, by Krzysztof Dydynski, and *Guide to Venezuela*, by Hilary Dunsterville Branch.

Since the Orinoco is linked to the Amazon River, and the Yanomami Indians of Venezuela are part of the Yanomami people of Brazil, I read "Yanomamo" by Napoleon A. Chagnon, a French cultural anthropologist, in *Primitive Worlds: People Lost in Time*, by the National Geographic Society. *Yanomamo of the Orinoco*, a videotape by Timothy Asch and Napoleon Chagnon, is available for school rental. A good videotape about the Amazon rain forest, which extends into Venezuela, is *Amazon: Land of the Flooded Forest*, by the National Geographic Society.

On the Internet, I found articles about the Orinoco River from the Earthwatch Research Society. An excellent resource was the April 1998 issue of *National Geographic* magazine. I also found that the rain forest, tepuis and Angel Falls, and the Yanomami were featured on television's Discovery, Travel, and PBS channels. A CD-ROM about Christopher Columbus's expeditions provided useful information about the first European to explore the Orinoco River.

Just for fun and "flavor"—but not for facts because sometimes storytellers make them up—I read the three classic stories about the river and the region: *Robinson Crusoe*, by Daniel DeFoe, *Green Mansions*, by W. H. Hudson, and *The Lost World*, by Sir Arthur Conan Doyle. *Dragons in the Waters*, by Madeleine L'Engle, is a good, more recent, mystery about Simón Bolívar and the Venezuelan rain forest.

—*Carol B. Rawlins*

Index

Numbers in *italics* indicate illustrations.

Amazonas Territory, 15,
    29–33, *30*, *31*, *32*
    access to, 43
Amazon River, 23, 27, 32,
    38–39, 41
Andes Mountains, 12, 20,
    23, 44
Angel, Jimmy, 16
Angel Falls, *16*
Angostura, 48
Animals, 30–32, *30*, *31*, *32*,
    46
Apure River, 44, 45
Atlantic Ocean, *18*, 20, 23,
    38, 52, *52*, 53
Atures Rapids, 40, 43

Barrancas, 53
Biosphere Reserve, 35
Black Gold, 26, *26*
Blue mountain, 38
Bolívar, Simón, 12, 48, *48*

Bolívar City, 21, *21*, 43, 44,
    45, 47–48
Books, 56–57
Brazil, 12
"Breadbasket" of Venezuela,
    45
Bridge across the Orinoco, 47

Caicara del Orinoco, 47
Canaima National Park, 17
Canoe people, 9
Capybara (rodent), 46, *46*
Caracas, 13, 43
Carib people, 25
Caroní River, 15, 48, 49
Casiquiare Channel, 27,
    37–39, *38*
Caura River, 47
Climate, 17, 44–45
Colombia, 12, 20, 39–40, 44
Columbus, Christopher, *24*,
    26

Continents, 9

Dams, 22, *22*, 49–50, *50*
Deltas, 51–53, *52*
Discharge, measuring, 20
Drainage area, 20

Electric eel, 32
Explorers, *24*, 26–27, *27*,
    29–30

Fierce people. *See* Yanomami
    people
Future, 53

Gold, 35
Gran Sabana, 15, 17, 49
Guajiro people, 33
Guaviare River, 40
Guayana City, 49–50, *49*, 53
Guayana Shield, 14
Guiana Highlands, 14–17,
    15, *16*, 44, 47, 49
Guri Dam, 22, *22*, 49–50, *50*
Guyana, 12

Humboldt, Alexander von,
    27, 39

Indigenous people, 33

Industrial development, 8, *8*,
    22, 49–50, *49*, *50*

La Esmeralda, *36*, 37
Lake Maracaibo, 12, *26*, 33
Llaneros, 14, *14*, 21, 46–47
Llanos, 20, 44–47, *45*, *46*,
    50, *51*

Macagua Dam, 22
Maipures Rapids, 40
Makiritare people, 33
Map, *10*
Meta River, 44
Mount Duida, 38

National parks, 17
Negro River, 38, 39

Oil, 12, 26, *26*, 53
Ojeda, Alonso de, 26
Online sites, 58
Organizations, 58
Orinoco River, *9*
    flow, direction, 23
    length, *9*, 11
    lower river, 8, *8*, 43–50,
        45, *46*, *49*, *50*
    map, *10*
River Basin, 20–22, *21*, 45

source, 29
upper river, 37–41, *38,
    40–41*
water quality, 22–23

Parrots, *30*, 31
Pemon Indians, 17
People
    indigenous people, 33
    population of Venezuela,
        17
Piaroa people, 33
Pico Bolívar, 12, *12–13*
Plants, 23, 32, 35
Poison, 35
Port Ayacucho, *42*, 43–44, 47

Rain forest, 7, 12, 15, 23, *23,
    28. See also* Amazonas
    Territory
Rapids, 40–41, *40–41*
Reclaiming land, 53
Rio Grande, 53

San Fernando de Atabapo,
    40
Seasons, 8, 17

Snakes, 31–32, *31*

Tapir, 32, *32*
Television, 57
Tepuis, 15–17, *15, 16*

Venezuela, 11–17, *15, 16*
    capital, 13
    fastest growing city, 49
    future, 53
    highest peak, *12–13*
    history of, 12
    population, 17
    size, 11
    War of Independence,
        48
Ventuari River, 39

Warao Indians, *6*, 7–8, 9,
    53
Waterfalls, *16*, 48

Yanomami people, 33,
    34–35, *34*, 39
Yekwana people, 25, 33–34,
    36

About the Author

Carol Blashfield Rawlins has deep midwestern roots. Born in Wisconsin, she attended public schools in Illinois, graduated from Ohio Wesleyan University, and then returned to Illinois to teach high school English, history, and social studies. Later she moved to Topeka, Kansas, where she raised a daughter and son, attended graduate school at the University of Kansas, and worked for the State of Kansas.

A Californian for more than a decade, Carol and her husband live in Santee. They are what the *Los Angeles Times* calls "water people," which means they are fascinated with all the Earth's rivers. The Rawlinses plan their vacations around rivers because they enjoy following them from beginning to end and documenting what they see along the way.

Ms. Rawlins is also the author of *The Colorado River* for Franklin Watts.